906-090-ΛꞰ

THE LONDON FILE
PAPERS FROM THE INSTITUTE OF EDUCATION

THE AIMS OF SCHOOL HISTORY:
THE NATIONAL CURRICULUM AND BEYOND

PETER LEE, JOHN SLATER,
PADDY WALSH and JOHN WHITE
with a preface by DENIS SHEMILT

INSTITUTE OF
EDUCATION
UNIVERSITY OF LONDON

Published by

the Tufnell Press

PUBLISHED
by
the Tufnell Press
47, Dalmeny Road, London, N7 0DY

All Rights reserved. No part of this publication may be reproduced, stored in a retrieval system, or transmitted in any form or by any means, electronic, mechanical, photocopying, recording or otherwise, without the prior permission of the publisher.

© 1992, Peter Lee, Denis Shemilt, John Slater, Paddy Walsh and John White

First published 1992
Reprinted October 1993

BRITISH LIBRARY CATALOGUING-IN-PUBLICATION DATA
A catalogue record for this book is available from the British Library

ISBN 1 872767 26 5

UNIVERSITY OF HERTFORDSHIRE
LIBRARY, WALL HALL CAMPUS
CLASS
HL 00876954
907 Aim
COLLECTION/LOAN STATUS
ITEM
1- 872767-26-5

Book design by Fiona Barlow, Carter Wong, London
Printed in Great Britain by Da Costa Print, London

CONTENTS

PREFACE

Denis Shemilt

To teachers grappling with the minutiae of National Curriculum orders and assessment regulations, discussion about the aims and purposes of history teaching may seem as stale and profitless as speculation about the length of Cleopatra's nose—fit matter for senior common rooms but with no purpose else. This perception is one of the dangers and, perhaps unavoidable penalties of a National Curriculum which may do for history teaching what the Donation of Constantine did for Christianity. I recently supervised teaching practice in a school that had 'solved' the National Curriculum by devising a history syllabus in which Programmes of Study had been broken down into blocks of seven lessons with every eighth lesson being used to 'knock off' a Statement of Attainment. Intended learning outcomes were formally divorced from prescribed historical content and the aim of the whole had degenerated into a mechanical compliance with bureaucratic regulations. National Curriculum Attainment Targets and Programmes of Study, statutory orders and non-statutory guidance, constitute a series of landmarks and compass bearings which may prove of value if you know where you are, where you are going and why you wish to get there. In the absence of a clear sense of purpose which, alas, is not immanent within the National Curriculum, they define an educational etiquette not an ethic, and are ineluctably trivial. As observed by the self-styled Comte de Lautreamont, 'If Cleopatra's morality had been less free, the face of the earth would have changed. But her nose wouldn't have become any longer.'

Many questions about the aims and purposes of history teaching have, in fact, been answered by the National Curriculum: along with other foundation subjects and religious education, it should promote 'the spiritual, moral, cultural, mental and physical development of pupils' and prepare them 'for the opportunities, responsibilities and experiences of adult life' (Education Reform Act, 1988). From this in follows that the aims of history should relate to the potentialities of the individual as well as to the needs of society, and must be broadly civilising rather than narrowly instrumental. A number of questions are left unanswered, however, and these are addressed and debated by the contributors to this London File pamphlet. The four most important questions may be summarised as follows.

1. How should the aims and purposes of history teaching relate to the aims and purposes of education, 5-16?

This question assumes a variety of forms. Are the aims of history teaching a subset of the aims of education 5-16? Are these peculiar to history or common to one or more other subjects? Do different subjects fulfil common aims in similar or dissimilar ways, i.e. do they reinforce or complement each other? Might history teaching have aims superogatory to those of the basic curriculum? Answers to each question depend upon the prior explication of the fundamental relationship between the aims of the whole and the aims of the parts, between the basic curriculum and its constituent subjects. Are the aims of the basic curriculum 5-16 a generalised summation of subject aims *or* are individual subject aims instantiations of basic curriculum aims? Differences in the philosophies and formats of subject orders, the exclusion of religious education from the regulatory framework of Attainment Targets and Programmes of Study, and the half-way house treatment of cross-curricular themes suggest that neither relationship obtains, that there is no intellectually coherent or practically workable relationship between individual subject and whole curriculum aims. Whether or not such a relationship can and, if so, should be separately invented by teachers of each and every basic curriculum subject are questions that remain.

2. Is it possible to formulate aims for history teaching, 5-16?

History is now an elective subject for the 14-16 age group. This, in itself, may pose no insuperable difficulties for the definition of the aims and purposes of history 5-16. More problematic is the fact that history 14-16 may take a number of forms: 100 per cent or 50 per cent Key Stage 4 history; history as a free-standing subject or as part of a hybrid course in conjunction with geography or business studies, or whatever—and be assessed by means of GCSE or of some as yet undeveloped prevocational courses. Clearly the aims and purposes of history 14-16, in its 100 per cent GCSE version, will be co-extensive and commensurable with those for history 5-14, but it is far from clear that this will follow for abbreviated and hybrid courses.

3. To what extent should history teaching aim to develop pupils' understanding of the methodological basis of the discipline?

At issue here is the primacy of Attainment Targets or of Programmes of Study. At one extreme, the purpose of history is to inform pupils about certain bits of 'the past' and Attainment Targets do no more than facilitate assessment of this knowledge by allowing for the fact that some pupils will master, for example, Key Stage 2 content at higher levels than will other pupils addressing Key Stage 3 content. Attainment Targets, according to this view, are a mechanical device permitting differentiation in the teaching and learning of prescribed history study units. At the other extreme, history teaching should aim to develop pupils' mastery of more generally useful concepts and skills. From this it follows that Programmes of Study are no more than vehicles for developing this mastery and for teaching to Attainment Targets interpreted as hierarchies of transferable skills. This debate antecedes the National Curriculum and has led to more schisms and heresies than did the seventeenth century. Proponents of methodological history tend to split between advocates of 'generalisable skills' on the one hand and, on the other hand, those who argue that pupils' capacity to make personal sense of and to benefit from study of the past is conditional upon their understanding of historical claims to knowledge, of the nature of historical accounts and of the logic of the several forms of historical explanation. Constructivist analyses of pupils' thinking have, in recent years, done much to expose 'the past in pupils' heads' to the scrutiny of their teachers. Sometimes these analyses reveal simplistic misconceptions, as with the Year 7 pupil who thought that the Romans lived two metres underground. Sometimes, misconceptions result from inappropriate transfer of schemata from other subjects, as with Year 11 pupils who reasoned that historical 'causes' could be cancelled or compensated by other 'contra-' or 'counter-causal' events, as in elementary mechanics. Other misconceptions are more deep-rooted. For example, many pupils have difficulty in accommodating to the uncertainty and provisionality of historical accounts because they fail to distinguish the two questions, 'What is the case?' and 'What are we entitled to say about the case?' Until they learn how to determine what it is 'valid to assert' rather than to seek what is 'true in fact', the admission that an historical account might be in error is tantamount to asserting that it is guesswork with no especial claim to serious consideration. Anyone can guess or give an opinion!

The argument that the methodology or 'logical grammar' of the subject needs to be explicitly taught rather than just 'picked up' is strong, but begs the question of what content is to be taught. It is difficult to claim that methodology must be taught in order for pupils to make good sense of the past if no statement follows as to which 'past' they should encounter. There is consensus that study of the past should be both 'broad' and 'balanced', but significant dissension as to how broad and in what way balanced. Especially vexed are debates about the dividing line between the historical past and current affairs, about the relevance of ancient and medieval history, about heritage versus world history, about political versus socio-economic history, and—most contentious of all—about 'people's history' versus that of political and economic élites. Less frequently debated is the desirability and feasibility of teaching pupils an outline of human history as an alternative or in addition to a selection of 'lines' and 'patches'. The arguments in favour of a conspectus of history in its entirety are compelling and it is surprising that commentators seeking to increase the proportion of recent, world, or whatever, history within a modified National Curriculum should have paid them so little attention.

If we discount arguments in favour of history as a curricular vehicle for teaching generalisable skills and competencies, which arguments are often, though not exclusively associated with the TVEI lobby; and if we also discount arguments in favour of history as a received account of the past, as advocated by the extreme political right and, in the Seventies, by the extreme left also, we are left with a debate which focuses upon the extent to which history teaching should aim for methodological understanding, for conspectual knowledge of the shape of human history, and for more detailed knowledge of various bits of the past. These questions cannot be answered in isolation from Section 4. below.

4. In what ways should study of the past aim to be relevant to pupils' present and future lives?

There is, of course, a school of thought that history should be taught to *all* 5-16 year olds for no reason other than that it is a humane and worthwhile thing to do. Similar arguments are used to justify the teaching of English literature, But this sort of justification is more appropriate to studies that are personally selected rather than those that are socially compelled, and it may be dangerous to allow our fascination with the past to displace consideration of present concerns lest, as with Yeats in later life, we eventually lament that 'players and painted stage took all my love/and not those things that they were emblems of'.

4

Most teachers and commentators would agree that, if history teaching does not make the generality of pupils in some way 'better' and benefit society as a whole, then it is nothing of consequence. The question remains as to what sort of 'improving subject' history should aim to be. For example, should history aim to promote in pupils a reasoned commitment to liberal democracy, a principled loathing of racism, a fervent patriotism, or what? Most people would agree that history teaching which, for the generality of pupils, nourished anti-democratic behaviour or led to closed and bigoted minds would undermine the sort of society necessary for humane and critical history teaching to flourish. St. Augustine argued that God can only be defined by means of negative statements; whatever our muddied souls and myopic minds can conceive, God is not. In like manner, it is convenient to define the aims of history teaching in negatives: good history teaching is the enemy of the undemocratic, the bigoted, the irrational and the cruel.

Such aims are convenient, but are they satisfactory? Why cannot we say that we aim to promote in pupils a positive adherence to liberal democracy or a clean-cut and sturdy patriotism? Of course we can do so, but only if we are prepared to say where democracy begins—in the home, the workplace, Westminster, or Strasbourg—and where patriotism ends—the EC, the nation state or in the proposed regional parliaments. We must also be prepared to say what answers history suggests to these and other questions or, if we are honest, to pervert the subject to particular propagandist ends. Like the Bible, the past can be pressed into any devil's service, used selectively and persuasively to prove any case.

An alternative aim of history teaching would be to induct pupils into a debate about what democracy and patriotism can and should be. In broad terms, history teaching might aim to sustain an 'open society' by initiating pupils into an 'open tradition', a tradition based first and foremost upon a critical and evidence-based examination of its own past and a cold-eyed recognition that social, political and economic forms, ideas and values change and develop in ways that elude millenarian blueprints and golden-age atavisms. Rather than promote commitment to some particular version of democracy, perhaps we should aim to teach pupils that democracy has been and meant many things and that what it may be will depend upon, though not be determined by, what people now wish it to be. Rather than enhance patriotism, perhaps we should aim to give pupils a sense of the heroism and the tragedy of human endeavour, of the nobility and sacrifice of human aspirations co-mingled with the self-delusion of unenlightened self-interest and the gross comedy of unintended consequences. Perhaps pupils so taught will be equipped to make free and knowing choices within the open tradition of which critical history is a part. But they might be no more patriotic nor committed to definitions of democracy which their teachers own!

This debate on the aims and purposes of history teaching is potentially significant in that teachers who espouse PSE-type aims like 'commitment to democracy' and the 'promotion of patriotism' will be disposed to stress content over methodology, Programmes of Study over Attainment Targets, and will tend to select syllabus content and learning materials pertinent to those aims. On the other hand, teachers who espouse 'open tradition' aims (what Peter Lee terms 'transformative aims') will afford explicit emphasis to historical methodology and be concerned to teach as comprehensive a conspectus of human history as possible within the framework of the National Curriculum.

* * *

Although none of the four contributors to this London File would claim to have delivered the last word about the aims and purposes of history within the existing or a reformed National Curriculum, each offers ideas and arguments which, in one way or another, enrich what must remain an ongoing debate.

John White explodes a number of all too familiar distinctions between 'extrinsic' and 'intrinsic' aims, and between 'instrumental history' and 'history for its own sake', more clearly and decisively than any previously commentator. He also illuminates the distinction between 'value-free' history, a rainbow's end ideal, and 'interest-free' history, the basis of objective scholarship.

Perhaps the single most intellectually powerful idea to emerge from these essays is Peter Lee's postulation of an uncertainty principle articulating the relationship between the sorts of history that may be taught and the purposes that history teaching may serve. If I understand Lee aright, he claims (1) that while methodologically informed and critical history teaching is likely to transform pupils' apprehension of human and social possibilities, the nature of such transformations, in terms of the social, political and economic values and beliefs which pupils espouse, will be uncertain. Pupils' ideas about democracy may change or be reinforced, but cannot be predicted. Transformations of whatever kind are worthwhile if more rational, based upon a more informed acknowledgement of alternative possibilities, more sceptical about what passes as 'facts' and self-evident truths, and more suspicious of dogma. In Lee's view, the sort of transformation that history teaching should aim to effect is definable in quality but uncertain in kind.

Lee's reciprocal proposition is (2) that the history teaching which aims to promote prespecified ideas and values about market economies, multiculturalism, liberal democracy, nation-state patriotism, or whatever, is of uncertain moral and intellectual integrity. Lee is careful not to claim that a history subordinated to PSE purposes must necessarily fall into intellectual corruption. It is just that its purity cannot be guaranteed. We can answer for the history or for the outcomes, but not for both—hence the uncertainty.

Paddy Walsh's distinction between 'pre-critical' and 'critical' history seems to be consistent with Lee's uncertainty principle. He also argues for the primacy of methodological aims in asserting that, at bottom, the 'only real difference' between pre-critical and critical history is that the latter is 'more concerned with getting the story right, and is methodologically better equipped to achieve...that fidelity'. His linking of critical history with 'piety' is reminiscent of Piaget's dictum that 'logic is the morality of mind'. Concern with the evidential basis of claims to knowledge, with the developmental logic of historical accounts, and with the modal logic of causal explanation is not mandarin pedantry; on the contrary, it is a moral concern fundamental to the maintenance of an open tradition, and, thereby, of an 'open society'.

John Slater's focus upon 'doubt' encapsulates in a word the aims and purposes of history teaching. In an era of conviction politics, it is perhaps unfortunate that 'doubt' possesses negative, and even wimpish, connotations. The sort of doubt properly engendered by history teaching, however, is not to be equated with vacillating indecision, but rather with a robust acknowledgement of the provisionality of assumptions, of the fragility of generalizations, and of the contestability of accounts. At the most elementary level, pupils must appreciate Willie Whitelaw's joke that 'one should not prejudge the past'. Doubt must inform our methodology, for we can never aspire to 'tell it like it was', only to work out what we are 'most justified in saying about the past', and even this may prove elusive when contrary statements seem to possess an equal validity. Doubt must also be engendered about the present and the future. Such doubt must follow not only from recognition of unintended consequences, but also from the realisation that we now view our past very differently from how many of our predecessors would have regarded their future, and what we choose to construe as progress our predecessors might have deemed a descent into vice, anarchy and impiety. We may stand in like relation to our successors, or even to ourselves a few decades removed. We may inch towards Jerusalem, but each forward movement brings fresh doubts about its nature and its bearings. Without such doubts we may stumble into Babylon. As was somewhat unkindly said of Plato on the failure of his philosopher-king experiments in Syracuse, 'one only has to be sufficiently determined to realise heaven on earth to be sure of raising hell'.

To doubt what is, what can be and what ought to be, is perhaps the greatest gift of historical study. To doubt, and to doubt without flinching, is to grow up. The four essays in this London File contribute to our maturity.

THE PURPOSE OF SCHOOL HISTORY: HAS THE NATIONAL CURRICULUM GOT IT RIGHT?

John White

History is a foundation subject in the National Curriculum. Why is it held to be important? How do its perceived purposes subserve the more general aims of the National Curriculum itself?

In this essay I shall argue that the answers to these questions point to lack of clarity and sense of direction. I shall suggest a new approach to them, based on a more rigorous examination of the issues at stake.

The shift to a National Curriculum in 1988 was a momentous change for schools in England and Wales. One might have expected the fundamental aims and values on which it rests to have been thoroughly worked out and then close attention paid to what those aims require in the way of more determinate aims, including aims in specific areas of understanding, e.g. historical.

But that is not what has happened. The aims of the National Curriculum as a whole are laid out with extraordinary brevity. The Educational Reform Act merely says that the school curriculum must be 'balanced and broadly based', promote 'the spiritual, moral, cultural, mental and physical development of students at school and of society' and prepare them 'for the opportunities, responsibilities and experiences of adult life'. Nothing can be derived from these empty imperatives about more determinate objectives. What, if anything, is required in students in the way of personal qualities, an understanding of science, a love of the arts? We do not know, because the general aims point us in no particular direction.

We do not know, among other things, what, if any, *historical* understanding is desirable. If all the weight were to be put on preparation for adult life, would this point to history courses harnessed to the demands of citizenship (however interpreted)? Or would it also cover a love of history as an option pursued for its own sake? We simply cannot tell. Neither do we know how preparation for adult life is to be related to the promotion of spiritual, moral, cultural, mental, and physical development, nor, indeed, what the latter terms might mean. Would it be officially acceptable for history courses to be wholly devoted the pursuit of history for its own sake as distinct from objectives to do with wider concerns like the promotion of patriotic attitudes or democratic citizenship? Again, no answer is evident.

The History Working Group which prepared the framework for history in the National Curriculum thus got no guidance from these overall aims about which directions to follow. They were on their own.

What were their recommendations and priorities? Both their Interim Report (DES, 1989) and Final Report (DES, 1990) lay out 'the purposes of school history' as *lists* of aims, but with no attempt at prioritising them—unless we read the order in which the items are presented as an order of importance. For the most part these can be divided into two categories:

(1) personal and social aims to do with the pupils' sense of identity, cultural roots and shared inheritances, and an understanding of other countries and cultures in the modern world;

(2) aims intrinsic to the subject to do with arousing interest in the past, disciplined enquiry and a grasp of historians' methodology.

Are there any clues about how the Working Group weighted (1) as against (2)? In the Interim Report the first three items belong to, indeed constitute, (1). The main difference in the Final Report is that arousing interest in the past, which belongs to (2), is given precedence over these three. It looks as if an original emphasis on personal and social aims was weakened in the end in favour of a somewhat more 'intrinsic' stance. But all this is speculation since, as I have implied, no *reasons* are given in either document to support one set of aims over another.

I shall argue later that this failure to argue out priorities helped to make the framework which the Working Group produced radically unsatisfactory. But in order to show this it is first necessary to broach the task ducked both by the framers of the National Curriculum in general and by the History Working Group in particular, that is, a reasoned assessment of the relative importance of different aims of school history.

Someone who *has* tackled this is Peter Lee (1984, 1991). He mounts a case for the study of history for its own sake instead of as a means to something else (Lee, 1991, pp 39-44).

There are several ways, in Lee's view, in which the study of history might figure as a means. One can impart a knowledge of the past in order to reinforce patriotism. This aim is not necessarily illegitimate: what is is the use of history for this purpose, since 'this runs counter to criteria of detachment and impartiality built into genuine historical study' (p 41). Similarly, considerations to do with living in an increasingly interdependent world have led to demands for 'world history', but again the basis of such proposals lie 'in political concerns extrinsic to teaching history' (p 42). In general, therefore, 'the reason for teaching history in school is not so that pupils can use it for making something else, or to change or preserve a particular form of society, or even to expand the economy. The reason for teaching history is not that it changes society, but that it changes pupils; it changes what they see in the world, and how they see it' (p 43).

This brings us to what Lee means by his preferred aim of 'history for its own sake'. 'History changes our whole view of the world, of what the present is and of what human beings are and might be' (p 42). It 'expands our whole picture of the world and of what ends might be possible' (p 43).

An initial problem here is: is it right to contrast this kind of transformative aim with instrumental aims where history is a means to something else? Is not the transformative aim equally instrumental, since from the educators' point of view children are being taught the subject *in order to* expand their picture of the world and of human beings? There are other means of doing this—literature, geography, science, for instance. Is not history one means among many?

The assumption which seems to lie behind the argument in Lee's 1991 that aims divide exclusively into intrinsic and extrinsic was questioned at one point in the remark in his earlier paper (Lee, 1984) that 'something that expands one's conception of the world does not fall exactly into either category' (p 13). What this suggests is that we need to dig below the bare intrinsic-extrinsic dichotomy to a more complex characterisation.

At the two extremes we may be able to find clear instances of intrinsic and extrinsic aims. To begin with the extrinsic. History lessons based heavily on rote learning of names and dates may be compulsory in a certain education system because these provide easily testable material to help select students for the next stage of schooling. Whether this practice occurs in fact is not relevant. The point is conceptual: in this example the goal for which history learning is a means could be served by any number of other possible means, e.g. spelling, basic arithmetic, lists of capes and bays or of Sanskrit verbs. There is no logical link between means and ends beyond the notion of easy testability.

At the intrinsic end we may, it seems, locate the study of history purely as an enjoyable activity. An example here might be a scholar at a university who immerses herself in the investigation of Anglo-Saxon penal systems. She is not doing this because she has bigger fish to fry about penal systems in general or the influence of pre-conquest on later practices: she is simply fascinated by her own delimited topic and its opportunities for the exercise of her professional skills.

I have turned to universities rather than schools because there are fewer complications in finding intrinsic examples. A school parallel might be a student who became fascinated by, say, the early history of railways and found herself intelligently delving further and further into the data, again in a delimited, self-contained way. The complication arises because, unlike the case of the university scholar, we are dealing in schools with people who are being *taught* the subject. From the teacher's point of view, *nothing* that he or she teaches is likely to be completely self-contained. If a lesson is about medieval castles, then while the teacher may well want the children to become wholly absorbed in the topic so that *from their point of view* they do the work for intrinsic reasons, *from the teacher's point of view* there are also larger purposes, embodied in the whole year's syllabus and the history curriculum of the school in its entirety, which this particular lesson subserves: insight into social stratification, an understanding of medieval Britain, respect for historical evidence, a love of history for its own sake (as distinct from absorption in a particular topic within history for its own sake).

If a teacher has such wider aims in mind, is she teaching a particular topic—like medieval castles—for extrinsic rather than intrinsic reasons? She certainly has reasons which go beyond the topic itself and in that sense they may be said to be extrinsic to it. Are all such extrinsic reasons *instrumental* reasons? That is, must we always be able to conceive the study of medieval castles as a means to some further goal? We have to make a distinction here. Let us take the examples of possible wider aims just mentioned. If the topic of medieval castles is studied in order to

12

develop an understanding of social stratification or respect for historical evidence or a love of history for its own sake, it is replaceable by other vehicles. In this respect (only) it is like the historical rote-learning of our earlier example which can be replaced by rote-learning in geography or Sanskrit. If, on the other hand, the wider aim is an understanding of medieval Britain, some grasp of the place of the castle in the government and economy of the country is indispensable. The topic is not a replaceable means to a further goal but a necessary and irreplaceable *part* of a wider whole.

There is also more to be said about replaceable elements. Suppose we take the example of work on the castle as a vehicle of encouraging respect for historical evidence. In one way this is different from using childrens' recalling historical dates by rote as a means of selecting them for different sorts of schooling. In both cases the content is replaceable in relation to the aim; but in the first case only the aim is *instantiated* in the content. That is, when they are working on the castle the children are encouraged to be sensitive to issues about evidence and so are acquiring skills and dispositions in this area which will be deepened over time. In this way—by instantiation—there is a *logical* link between goal and means. The same is not true of the rote-learning case since the aim of selection is not instantiated in the rote-learning.

So much for conceptual distinctions, especially those to do with part-whole relationships and with instantiation, which cast doubt on the adequacy of a simple intrinsic-extrinsic dichotomy in the aims of school history. What, now, about the substantive issue of what these aims should be?

Peter Lee favours the transformative aim—of expanding our picture of the world—over other aims like the promotion of patriotism, citizenship, a sense of international interdependence, social and economic change. We have seen difficulties in labelling the former 'intrinsic' and the latter 'extrinsic', since in all these cases lessons in history are being used as a vehicle for something outside themselves. It is better, perhaps, to examine different proposed aims on their own merits, without being overly concerned about how to classify them.

Why is the transformative aim to be preferred? There are problems about what this aim might mean, but let us leave those on one side for the moment. As far as I can see, Lee gives us no explicit reason for his preference. Embedded in his discussion, however, is the thought that when 'history' is harnessed to other than

13

transformative purposes it is distorted and so does not really count as history. He says, for instance, that imparting knowledge of the past in order to create or reinforce patriotism 'runs counter to criteria of detachment and impartiality built into genuine historical study' (p 41).

The point about something not counting as history is an important one. We can all agree, I take it, that the study of history depends on certain intellectual virtues—detachment and impartiality, and others also—which are absent, for instance, in the teaching of Nazi 'history' or in the rote-learning of names and dates. But I am not clear why it is only when it is harnessed to the transformative aim that students are learning (genuine) history and not some ersatz version of it. Take citizenship as an aim. Suppose we have in mind the need to prepare students to become informed members of a liberal-democratic political community, not necessarily in its present imperfect form. For this they will need to understand our democratic institutions and the values on which they rest. For this in turn they will need some historical understanding of how things have developed as they have and how it might have been otherwise. I see no reason why the history they study for this reason cannot be genuine history, pursued with due regard for objectivity or impartiality.

The argument that all aims except the transformative are knocked out because only transformative reasons can lie behind genuine history teaching thus falls. Non-transformative aims are still in the ring.

All this supposes that we know what we mean when talking about transformative aims. But what is it, after all, to change a person's 'view of the world, of what the present is and of what human beings are and might be' (p 42)? This aim, we should remember, is being set against aims like the promotion of patriotism and citizenship. Yet in nurturing the democratic citizen is one not changing the way the student sees the world—so that what must seem to a young person the bewildering hullabaloo surrounding general elections, for instance, takes shape as having developed out of various traditions and practices? Perhaps what Lee has in mind is that while changing one's picture of the world is involved in all sorts of possible aims like citizenship, socialisation, patriotism or maintaining or changing society, in all the cases mentioned the transformation is part of, or on the way to, some larger purpose. In rejecting this, Lee must, it seems, be saying that changing one's view of the world is important in itself, without any further rationale.

This brings us, perhaps, to the heart of what Lee means by upholding the study of history for its own sake. The content of any particular history lesson, or series of lessons, including the history curriculum of a school as a whole, must be seen as serving some purpose or other which lies outside the lesson or series itself. In that sense it has an extrinsic purpose or purposes. But it could be that when we come to one or other of these extrinsic purposes we find that it is seen as important not for any further purpose that lies beyond it, but for its own sake. This seems to be so of Lee's transformative aim.

But why is changing one's picture of the world important in itself?—And how, in any case, are we to understand this aim? Would it justify a school history curriculum's being devoted for all five or six years of its duration to medieval England, or ancient India, or the Roman Empire (or a combination of these and similar items) since any of these variants may well transform how one sees the world and human nature? We will return to this issue later in connection with the National Curriculum.

To come back to the justification for making transformation important for its own sake. In the work of Richard Peters we find a similar claim. In Peters' case this kind of aim becomes definitional of 'education': this is seen as an initiation into various forms of understanding deemed important for its own sake. On this view, if history is being taught as a vehicle of citizenship and not for its own sake, this lies outside the enterprise of education. Possibly Lee is relying on some such move: it would certainly make sense of his whole position. But it would be unwise to do so, for there is no reason why we must accept such a definition of 'education'. Adjudication between aims cannot be short-circuited by defining certain of them—in this case non-intrinsic ones—out of bounds (See White, 1982, ch. 2). They all have to be reasoned through.

I have argued elsewhere (White, 1982, ch. 2 and White, 1990, ch. 7) that no good reasons have been put forward for making the expansion of understanding or knowledge for its own sake a basic objective in education. This argument applies to the transformative aim as an end in itself in history teaching in particular. This still allows a place for it as a *non*-basic objective within a larger setting. In White (1990) I advocate the promotion of the student's well-being as an autonomous person within a liberal-democratic community as a central aim in education, making it clear that, on the interpretation I give of this, a person's personal flourishing embraces a concern for others' flourishing in both more intimate and more impersonal contexts. One aspect of being an autonomous, i.e. self-directed, person in the conduct of one's life is that one uncoercedly chooses one's route through life (within evident constraints, to be sure) from options available to one. These cover such areas as jobs, residence, sex and family life, politics, leisure activities. One function of schooling should be to open up these various options. Among the options—both as leisure activities and as entering into possible careers—are forms of academic study pursued for their own sake. These have no privileged place as life-options above non-academic pursuits, but even so there is a strong case for introducing students to them while still at school. In this way, the study of history for its own sake (which includes its transformational benefits) can and should be one of a school's aims, just as much as the study of mathematics or literature for their own sakes.

What *weight* should be put on this reason for teaching history is another matter, for the autonomy aim brings with it other and arguably more important requirements on the subject. Take again the school's role in opening up life-options in jobs, politics, leisure and other areas. Understanding the range of options in these areas has an ineluctable historical dimension: one has only to think of the changes in patterns of employment over the last century, the coming of a universal franchise including votes for women, reductions in working hours and the expansion of leisure industries. Not only this: history is also indispensable in making us aware of the key role of the value of personal autonomy in modern conceptions of personal well-being—by contrast with pre-modern societies (and various religious communities within our larger society), in which tradition-directed expectations structured much more closely the way individuals were to live.

Awareness of options is only one part of becoming personally autonomous. One also has to understand the social worlds—from the family through to local, national and supranational communities—within which one's autonomous life will be lived, bearing in mind the altruistic as well as more exclusively self-regarding concerns built into the present conception of autonomy. There is no need to labour in the context of this paper the essential role that history plays in promoting this understanding. Because we are dealing here with the very framework of our lives, as distinct from choices made within that framework as described in the last paragraph, it is in this area that school history can make its most fundamental contribution to overall aims.

One aspect of this last point is that a historical dimension is essential to self-understanding, itself a vital ingredient in anyone's leading a flourishing life. To understand oneself is among other things to understand the complex web of often conflicting values by which one governs one's life. These values are not something one invents oneself, even though as an autonomous person one to some extent imposes one's own weightings on them. They are taken over from the social worlds in which one is brought up and belong to traditions of thought, feeling and behaviour which stretch back into the past. Ideals of civic humanism deriving originally from the Greeks, Christian inwardness, the privileging of the ordinary life of workplace and family that has come down to us from seventeenth century nonconformism, the values of scientific detachment and universal beneficence associated with the Enlightenment, the central place given to artistic creativity in the Romantic and post-Romantic reaction to the Enlightenment—all these and other traditions have helped to shape the milieux and communities within which we live and to make us as individuals living in mainstream Anglo-American culture what we are. In the title of Charles Taylor's recent (1989) book on the subject, they are all 'sources of the self'. More, of course, would need to be said about cultures and sub-cultures outside this mainstream.

A word in this connection on patriotism. Lee eschews it as a reason for teaching history. If he has in mind the chauvinism associated, for instance, with myths of British superiority and imperial power, we can only agree with him. But in Britain as in other industrialised countries, a major social framework for our lives is provided by our national community. As future autonomous, other-regarding democratic citizens, children need to be brought up with a certain degree of attachment to this larger polity which makes such a way of life possible. They must see themselves as bound to other members of the community by common ties, including shared mores, a shared history and—to some extent—a shared language. As David Miller (1988) has recently argued, a democratic society needs such common bonds in order to flourish, and the nation provides one such locus for them. This notion of the nation need not be tied to national superiority. As an 'imagined community' (Anderson, 1983), it can be shaped by quite other ideals, the values of democracy, freedom, tolerance and impartiality, for instance. Although British history has been redolent with oppressions of all kinds, there is at the same time some truth in the picture we sometimes have of ourselves as a seedbed of political freedom, tolerance, and beneficence towards the socially deprived. I see no harm, and much good, if school history traced for us the roots of our democratic traditions as an explicit contribution to the growth of a sense of British nationhood.

This does not at all mean ignoring the underside of cruelties and injustices, since these themselves are part of the story of our democracy. Neither need it mean deviating from the historian's virtues of objectivity and impartiality: indeed, these very virtues can be imparted as (broadly) the Enlightenment's contribution to the formation of our national identity as I am suggesting it might be shaped.

To conclude this part of the argument. I have been filling out a conception of school history which locates its place in a wider picture of educational aims. If we refer back to the two kinds of aim proposed by the History Working Group, we have now got grounds for according priority to the personal and social aims rather than methodological aims intrinsic to the discipline. The two kinds of aim are not of the same order of importance. It should be *taken as read* that the intrinsic aims (in this sense of 'intrinsic') will be met, simply because it is history with which we are concerned and not music or technology: just as attention to the logical cogency of proofs is not a reason for teaching mathematics but rather a part of what it is to teach the subject, so disciplined enquiry into the past is similarly constitutive of studying history and not an aim which lies behind it.

If the History Working Group had prioritised their aims along these lines instead of leaving things more open, would the Study Units which they worked out for different key stages have turned out differently? It is hard to say, of course, but what is striking about these Units, even before their later revision by the Secretary of State, is the little attention given to recent British—and to a lesser extent world—history. 'Britain in the twentieth century' constitutes a one-term compulsory course at Key Stage 4, occupying the same curricular space as 'Medieval Realms: c.1066 to c.1500' at Key Stage 3. If school history's main purposes are to promote self-knowledge and an awareness of the social framework of the autonomous life and choices within it, then it should surely be weighted more towards the last two hundred years and the emergence of industrialised societies. Of course all sorts of strands in our social and personal make-up have their origins in the remoter past, and school history should obviously reflect this. It is all a question of where the weight should fall. What I am suggesting is that the History Working Party gives every sign of having followed the conventional practice of history teachers both at school and university and given greater attention to chronological time-slicing than to what students most need from the point of view of their own flourishing.

The Working Group's failure sensibly to resolve the tension between personal/ social requirements on the one hand and professionals' *modi operandi* on the other was shown up starkly in January 1991 when the government changed the original National Curriculum arrangements for Key Stage 4. History, along with geography, now became an optional subject. This meant at first that those students of 14-16 who chose to do geography rather than history would leave school with no acquaintance with British or world history in the twentieth century. After protests, a compulsory Study Unit in 'The Causes of the Second World War' was written in at Key Stage 3. This still means, however, that young people can finish their education with no understanding of what has happened in their own society in the last hundred years; and that even those who continue history beyond 14 spend only one term on this.

I have been arguing in this essay that the main reason for teaching history in schools is as a necessary element in the cultivation of those personal qualities in students, like self-knowledge, self-determination and concern for the well-being of others, which fit them to be citizens of a liberal-democratic society. This is at odds both with the views of those who advocate that history should be only studied for its sake and with the fence-sitting caution of the History Working Group. It points to a far greater place being accorded to the history of the industrial age in school history than either of these groups would favour.

HISTORY IN SCHOOL: AIMS, PURPOSES AND APPROACHES
A REPLY TO JOHN WHITE

Peter Lee

The difficult part of education is to connect a coherent conception of what ought to be done with the realities of teaching and the educational context. Achieving a coherent conception means doing some philosophy; making the connection means understanding some history, in this case the history of history-teaching and the debate over the National Curriculum. Philosophy without a historical perspective stops short of engagement with the practical world: not so much the classic problem of the gearwheels of language idling, more a case of a slipping clutch.

John White has written a valuable paper on the purpose of school history, in which he attributes certain views to me. He raises a number of important issues, some of which I will discuss in the course of this reply, but I do not think that our disagreements are always quite what he believes they are. No doubt this is mainly because my arguments were not expressed as clearly as they might have been, but perhaps it is also because White does not set them firmly enough in the context of the recent history of history teaching. At the same time there are clearly some matters genuinely in dispute between us.

The nature of our disagreement is perhaps best brought out by the following passage in White's essay.

'It should be *taken as read* that the intrinsic aims (i.e. the methodological aims of the discipline) will be met, simply because it is history with which we are concerned and not music or technology ... disciplined enquiry into the past is ... constitutive of studying history and not an aim which lies behind it.'[1]

In the real world of the National Curriculum, the issue that White argues should be taken as read—what is constitutive of studying history in school—is precisely what is contested. The methodological aims of history were not 'taken as read'; on the contrary they were in dispute, and seemed likely to be excluded.

How could this have happened? Why were these aims, that *should* have been taken as read, a matter for dispute? It will be central to my argument that what happened in the debate over history is precisely the sort of thing that goes wrong when no distinction is made between different levels of aims, and when personal and social aims are accorded priority as aims of history.

John White's argument seems to be based on the following related propositions:

(1) the claim that history should be taught in schools 'for its own sake' will not do (passim);
(2) the assumption that aims divide exclusively into intrinsic and extrinsic is false (p.11);
(3) history does not need to be 'harnessed to' the transformative aim I espoused in my two papers (p.14), and such a transformative aim is inadequate (pp.14-15);
(4) history's transformative aims are not special: there are other transformative aims to which history may be harnessed (p.14);
(5) personal and social aims take priority over methodological aims intrinsic to the discipline (p.18).

My reply will be that I agree with (1) and (2), and that White is incorrect in thinking that I assert these claims in my papers; that (3) and (4) rest on confusions between different kinds of 'transformation'; and that (5) fails to distinguish between different levels of aims, and confuses 'life-options' with choices in education. I shall argue that White does not sufficiently take account of the historical context of the debate in his criticisms of the Working Party and NCC. Finally, I shall examine the suggestions for changes in the content of school history which, White argues, follow from his arguments about aims.

White thinks that I espouse the view that history should be taught 'for its own sake'. In *History in the National Curriculum* I argued that there is an interpretation of the slogan that history should be studied 'for its own sake' which 'makes a great deal of sense'.[2] The point of my chapter was not to espouse the notion of 'history for its own sake', but to show that a current approach to school history which was being linked by the political right and by certain academics with social engineering and absurdly simple-minded notions of 'relevance' had no such assumptions or implications. The reason for trying to make some sense of the slogan was to show that any sense it *could* be given undermined many of the claims its political exponents made about history education. Indeed it was those who most loudly asserted the slogan who were most ready to override whatever meaningful claims it made.

The danger inherent in the construction of a history National Curriculum was that a demand for a knowledge attainment target would lead to a detailed specification of historical knowledge, which would in turn lead to the establishment of official—even party—history: a story which would be learnt by children as *the* story. (There would also be severe practical effects on teaching and assessment.) While the political right accused school history of social engineering, they used the slogan of 'history for its own sake' in their own attempt to build dykes against change, and tried to tie history teaching to a narrow and simplistic notion of handing on the facts.[3] Some of these moves were buttressed by demands that history should pass on a heritage and re-inforce patriotism (in some cases understood in an almost xenophobic way). Hence it was important to establish that an approach to history teaching that went beyond the acquisition of information about the past to develop an understanding of the discipline did not entail the view that history should be a vehicle for political propaganda or social engineering. Far from weakening history, and turning it into something more akin to PSE, many of the recent developments in history teaching have toughened the conception of history as an academic discipline. In fact, the pressure to turn history into a vehicle came from another source. At the very moment when influential groups on the right were pressing the claim of heritage and demanding a simplistic emphasis on the acquisition of fact, those with a vocational bent, sometimes in alliance with industrialists and sometimes with elements of the political left, argued that history should be made 'useful', or be replaced in the curriculum with other subjects. Some headteachers had, prior to the advent of the National Curriculum, cut or even closed down flourishing history departments in favour of PSE.

In trying to salvage something useful from the slogan 'history for its own sake', I attempted to cut through some of these sets of assumptions in order to avoid being misrepresented by right or left. The passage that is closest to appearing to support the slogan in question runs as follows:

> The claim that history should be studied for its own sake is, then, a way of making two assertions: that history is not useful as a means to an end, but valuable as something which expands our whole picture of what ends may be possible; and that to have this value it must be genuine history, not the practical past in disguise.[4]

My interpretation of the slogan accepts that history is not useful on a technological model, and cannot be a practical subject: 'it has no skills or lessons which can be directly *applied* in clearly defined activities or to neatly demarcated classes of physical objects'.[5] The emphasis in the passage is on what White calls 'the transformative aim', a useful shorthand which I am happy to adopt.

The reason for teaching history in schools is not so that pupils can use it for making something else, or to change or preserve a particular form of society, or even to expand the economy. The reason for teaching history is not that it changes society, but that it changes *pupils*; it changes what they see in the world, and how they see it.[6]

The slogan 'history for its own sake' can, then, be used to make both negative and positive points: negatively, to rule out the use of history in schools for social engineering (of the left or right); positively, to stress the role of history in transforming the way in which pupils are able to see the world.

The central issue is the transformative aim. It is this which seems to be at the base of any disagreement between White's position and my own, and this which has practical consequences for what goes on in schools. But before I embark on a discussion of the transformative aim, it is worth stressing that I have no difficulty with White's formal elaboration of the concepts of extrinsic and extrinsic aim. (My own concern was in fact with extrinsic and intrinsic *criteria* for the construction of history curricula.) There are certainly differences between us about the way in which such aims are related to educational aims, but none—as far as I can tell—about the analysis of *extrinsic* and *intrinsic* as such. It is therefore odd that White should attribute to me the assumption that aims divide exclusively into intrinsic and extrinsic, and at the same time refer to a passage in which I point out that 'something that expands one's conception of the world does not fall exactly into either category'.[7] In any case White's main doubts about the transformative aim are not whether it is classified as intrinsic or extrinsic. They are that history does not need to be harnessed to the transformative aim, that *this* transformative aim has no special status, and that transformative aims of this kind are not enough.

White cannot understand 'why it is only when harnessed to the transformative aim that students are learning genuine history and not some *ersatz* version of it'. In the first place, history is not 'harnessed' to a transformative aim, precisely because the transformative aim is not (exclusively) extrinsic in this way. Teaching history in certain ways *is* bringing about the kind of transformation at issue: the transformation is not some further step. In the second place, it may well be that sometimes when history really is 'harnessed' to other aims, genuine history still takes place. The trouble is that if certain kinds of personal and social aims of the kind that White wants to claim should be aims of history are taken seriously, then whether history gets taught or some *ersatz* version of it is a matter of chance. It is not that without the transformative aim no genuine history can be taught, but that burdening history with personal and social aims which have priority over the transformative aim, or indeed over clearly intrinsic methodological aims, puts genuine history at risk. This is clear both on theoretical grounds, and in practice, in White's own handling of the matter.

One of White's reasons for thinking the transformative aim is not necessary is that it is instrumental, and that other instrumental aims are possible, for example patriotism or socialization.[8] Why should the way in which people see the world be changed in whatever way *history* changes it, rather than, say, in whatever way is needed for patriotism? (Note that this move ignores the fact that the transformative aim is not just instrumental, and, equally, not exclusively intrinsic or extrinsic.) But there is an important difference between teaching people to think historically and teaching them to be patriotic. Changing people's world-view through history is not the same sort of thing as changing their world-view through patriotism: one is a matter of enabling them to handle the whole of human experience in a particular way—broadly to offer them the prospect of a rational past—and the other is to get them to feel in a particular way about Britain.

History is a way of acquiring rational knowledge and understanding of the past—any or all of the past. And since the present, however specious, is, from the point of view of knowledge and understanding, rather short, history bears on much of what is construed as present. To say someone has learnt history is to say something very wide-ranging about the way in which he or she is likely to make sense of the world. History offers a way of seeing almost any substantive issue in human affairs, subject to certain procedures and standards, whatever feelings one may have. Patriotism, on the other hand, is a set of feelings and dispositions, underpinned by a cognitive (or sometimes quasi-cognitive) foundation consisting of substantive beliefs and values to which people subscribe, localized to a particular place and time. Being patriotic cannot be generalized. It makes no sense to educate people to be patriotic in general—towards America, Angola and Antigua, Belgium, Bolivia, Britain and Brazil ... and so on.

The change of view one acquires from history is not just a matter of picking up a new set of beliefs, or even new substantive knowledge. It is also taking on a set of second-order understandings, together with the 'rational passions' (e.g. for truth and respect for evidence) which give historical understanding a universality that patriotism does not have. Learning history is like learning science: it is transformative in a radically different way from becoming patriotic or even socialized. (Socialization arguably has a universal component, since all humans belong to societies. But any universal meanings which could be given to socialization would be either very abstract or very basic: socialization has to be socialization into some particular society.)

Another reason why White thinks the transformative aim is not necessary is that it is only one of a number of possible transformative aims. White's example of an alternative transformative aim is the nurture of democratic citizens. 'In nurturing the democratic citizen is one not changing the way the student sees the world ...?'[9] This is a more interesting example than patriotism, but still runs into the same kind of difficulty. Changing students' views by nurturing them as democratic citizens is very different from changing students' views by teaching them history. There is radical disagreement about what democracy includes and excludes, and what counts as being a democratic citizen will vary with the disagreements about the concept itself. While there are certainly disagreements within history, the notion of democracy is contested in a much more radical way: it may, in Gallie's phrase, be *essentially contested*.

It is not just that learning history and producing patriotism or nurturing democratic citizens are aims which belong to different categories; it is also that the relation of learning history to becoming patriotic or being likely to see the world from a democratic perspective is a contingent one: learning history has no necessary connection with becoming patriotic or seeing the world from a democratic perspective. It is perfectly possible for students to learn history and be less patriotic than they were before they began. (Indeed it is precisely the claim that this was what was happening in schools that led the far right to get so excited about history teaching.)

What aims can or should history have? A set of aims which omitted criterial achievements and mentioned only contingent ones would be inadequate and misleading. There is little point in going for aims which have no discernible connection with history: how can they be aims of *history* teaching? And among the many contingent aims which might be plausibly asserted to have *some* sort of connection with history, those which are not linked to history by decent empirical evidence have little claim to be taken seriously: they lie somewhere along the continuum running from pious hopes through self-deception to deliberate misrepresentation.

White imagines that patriotism can become an aim of history without any ill effects. But the idea that history can remain history (meet, for example, standards of detachment and impartiality, and be organized according to historical rather than practical criteria) and still have as an aim the creation of patriots is simply disingenuous. History does not, *qua* history, create patriots or even nurture democrats. The claim that history can have patriotism as a serious aim must admit to a willingness to distort history by doing whatever turns out to be necessary to create patriots, or remain a bogus aim, a mere unjustified hope.[10]

It might be argued that the aim of 'nurturing democratic citizens' is a much weaker aim than the creation of patriots. It is not that history must lead students to *becoming* democrats: nurturing democrats is just another transformative aim. As such it means giving pupils certain ways of approaching political and other questions. But what are these ways? No doubt they would include moral, sociological, philosophical, and also historical ways. History cannot in itself be responsible for *this* kind of transformation: philosophical or sociological (and even moral) transformations are not within the gift of history. If history can only play a part, what part can it play? At this point we are back to the transformative aim of history, and the claim that history's aim should be to nurture the democratic citizen fails to add to that transformative aim because it has no consequences. Clearly White wants to give the claim some consequences when he argues that the transformative aim of history is not sufficient. But once it is accepted that the nurture of democratic citizens is an aim with consequences beyond the transformative aim of history, then it (like patriotism) becomes either just a heady wish, or a serious threat to the nature of history.[11]

White thinks I reject the idea that transformative aims can have larger purposes. This, he supposes, must mean that I am saying that changing one's view of the world is important without any further rationale.[12] But the rationale for the transformative aim is to be found in unpacking that aim, showing how one's view of the world is changed by history (in terms of substantive knowledge on the one hand, and dispositions and second order concepts and understandings on the other). These changes reach outside history itself by opening up new possibilities for action, by changing a chaos of practical pasts into rational history, and, through vicarious experience, giving us some purchase, however slight, on the future—not so much by predicting what it will be like as by preventing it from ambushing us.[13] In this sense history opens up *everything*, and to say that this is to reject some larger purpose is very odd: there can hardly be a much larger purpose. My problem with White's account is that he wants to *narrow* this larger purpose by harnessing history to particular forms of social organization.

White does not accept that the transformative aim can be sufficient for history. He argues that personal and social aims take priority over methodological aims intrinsic to the discipline.[14] He insists that the expansion of understanding 'for its own sake' cannot be a 'basic objective' in education.[15] For White, 'a central aim in education' is 'the promotion of the student's well-being as an autonomous person within a liberal-democratic community'. 'An autonomous, i.e. self-directed, person ... uncoercedly chooses' his or her 'route through life (within evident constraints ...) from options available'. 'One function of schooling should be to open up these various options.' While the autonomy aim set out here allows the study of history 'for its own sake (which includes its transformational benefits)' to 'be one of a school's aims', it imposes 'more important requirements on the subject'.[16]

What is it for personal and social aims to 'take priority'? There is no automatic connection between learning history and increased autonomy in pursuing life options, except the connection which can only be elucidated by unpacking the historical understanding built into the transformative aim. Why should we assume that the knowledge required for autonomy is just the same as is needed to meet decent historical standards, particularly if the standards at issue are concerned with the *basis* of knowledge? People who score highly on historical understanding will not necessarily perform better in the autonomous pursuit of life-options: indeed it is possible that concern for truth and awareness of the complexities of making sense of the past (and of that part of the present appropriately understood historically) may inhibit effective autonomy and muddy choices between options. A more practical past, offering certainties in terms of which to justify certain features of the present (perhaps the past organized as the origins of liberal-democracy) might offer clearer choices, fewer destructive confusions.[17] If so, given the priority of personal and social aims, perhaps history should be overridden or abandoned in favour of PSE.[18]

27

The relation between history and individual life paths requires empirical investigation. We may have expectations here, but we cannot legitimately claim that this relationship can be the basis of an *aim* of history in school, because we cannot say anything secure about what the relationship is. To do so would again be to indulge in pious hopes: unless, of course, we set out to make sure history in schools is selected and organised in such a way as to ensure the desired outcome. I am not sure how this would be done (we do not know enough about the relationship) but it is clear that an aim of this kind, given priority over methodological aims intrinsic to the discipline, would, *pace* White's denial, at least *allow* the sacrifice of methodological aims in the event that empirical research suggested clashes between them. This, of course, is precisely what so often happens in the real world in many TVEI and PSE courses, under pressure from both the entrepreneurial right and the condescending left. It is also what teachers feared would happen to history in the National Curriculum.

A stronger case could be argued to the effect that anyone who has studied history is likely to have a better *basis* for identifying and distinguishing life options than anyone who has not. Here we are talking about grounds for allocating descriptions to life-options, historical knowledge of what life-options there have been, and the ability to recognize an option as practicable or not. This is fine so far as it goes, and takes us beyond doing history, but it does not take us outside the transformative aim of historical understanding. Any attempt to characterize the 'value added' simply unpacks or glosses the transformative aim. The *way* in which the basis for identifying and distinguishing life-options improves is that it becomes more historical.

White tends to use aims, objectives, reasons, purposes and functions interchangeably, and to slip back and forth between schooling, education and history in a disconcertingly fluid way. What does it mean to say 'the study of history for its own sake can and should be one of a school's aims'?[19] Earlier on the same page White argues that 'forms of academic study pursued for their own sake' have 'no privileged place as life-options above non-academic pursuits'. There seems to be a confusion here between getting children to *take up* history (as a 'life-option') and teaching it in schools. Taking up the study of history 'for its own sake' *may* be an aim of schools, or a purpose adopted by history teachers, but it is hard to imagine anyone seriously offering it as a universal aim of history teaching, a central reason for having history in the curriculum, or a main aim of education. Ignoring distinctions here between different levels of aim—aims of education, aims of history teaching, and the aims of a school—helps to disguise a confusion about doing history for its own sake, and learning it in an educational system which has, as an aim of history, the transformation of children's perceptions of the world through historical understanding (both as methodological, second-order understanding, and as particular substantive understanding). Ruling out, or de-prioritizing, the aim of getting children to do history 'for its own sake' as a life-option is utterly different from ruling out or de-prioritizing the transformative aim of changing pupils understanding of the world by teaching them history. The problem here is partly one of confusing history as a life-option with history as a way of seeing the world; partly it is one of confusing aims of education with other levels of aims.

History's aims stop with the transformative aim: but this is where *educational* aims begin. The transformative aim is a central *aim of* school history: that is, it is what school history should aim for, an achievement to work towards. To the extent that there is empirical evidence to suggest that such an achievement is possible, it offers a *reason* for history to be included in the school curriculum. Unpacked, it provides aims *in* the teaching of history. Unpacked still further, it allows the specification of *objectives* for teachers and pupils.

The importance of distinguishing between aims of history and aims of education becomes clear the minute one takes seriously White's 'central aim' of 'the promotion of the student's well-being as an autonomous person within a liberal-democratic community'.[20] This is a perfectly acceptable (if contestable) aim of education, but it cannot be an aim of history. History has no allegiance to 'liberal-democratic community' as an ideal.[21] It is concerned to explore communities of every kind, both in their own terms and in ours, where 'ours' is never to be taken as a single fixed perspective belonging to one nation, class, race, culture or community. It emphasises that any such ideal is in any case continuously undergoing change, and that for this and other reasons the label may encompass conflicting conceptions. If history is part of education, it can be expected to contribute to education, but this does not mean that 'the aims of history' are the same as 'the aims of education', and it does not mean that the latter may be transposed down from the level of education in general to the level of history in particular. Something can legitimately be an aim of education that cannot be an aim of school history, and history may contribute to education achieving its (legitimate) aims without claiming those aims as its own.

White and I agree about much of what is to be gained from the study of history: the disagreement comes in how it is to be treated, and how far one can go with it.[22] I want to confine the aims of history to what can be delivered by history, and hence stress the transformative aim, which carries with it such personal and social benefits as are built into learning history. White—if I understand him correctly—wants to include among the aims of history more general personal and social goals. These I would categorize as aims of education, because there is nothing in history—*qua* history—to guarantee their delivery. (Of course, in another sense, nothing is guaranteed in education, but what is at issue here is whatever comes with achieving success in learning a subject or being educated.)

The failure to distinguish between different levels of aims has practical consequences. In the first place, as already argued in connection with patriotism and democracy, there is a kind of Heisenberg principle of history at work here. If history is taught so that priority is given to shedding light on the present, to pointing up origins, to offering lessons, or to encouraging—let alone inculcating—political or moral attitudes, it ceases to be adequate history, and fails to deliver even what it legitimately offers. If priority is given to intrinsic historical aims, the transformation aim becomes a realistic possibility, and this in turn means that there is some chance of achieving the wider educational aims.[23]

In the second place White's practical recommendation for change in the history curriculum is based on the idea that the history of Britain in the last 200 years, and particularly its recent history, is under-represented, not on historical grounds, but because it deals with industrialized society, and hence offers more opportunities to achieve the personal and social aims which take priority. There are, of course, good reasons why pupils should learn recent history. It demonstrates the illusory nature of the boundary between past and present. It enables pupils to understand the limits on what is possible now. It illustrates the way in which much that appears to be contemporary can only be understood as past-referencing. And it offers continuous exemplification of the way in which the past is used to legitimate or discredit aspects of the present.

Nevertheless, the idea that recent history, or the history of the past 200 years which saw the growth of industrialized societies, is better suited to enabling pupils to live the autonomous life, and therefore must be weighted against earlier history, is based on a narrow conception of the way in which history contributes to personal and social awareness. It exemplifies the dangers of confusing aims of education with aims of history, and then prioritizing personal and social aims as if they were directly aims of history. This is brought out by asking the question 'Why 200 years?' Why not 47 (since the Second World War), or 20 (since the advent of information technology), or even 13 (the Thatcher period)? If the criterion is provided by pupils' need to study the framework in which the autonomous life is set, presumably the assumption is that the framework of the last 200 years was *like ours*, an industrial one, not an alien agricultural rural one. But if the framework is to be like ours in that way, why go back so far?

Once we operate with some simple criterion of recognizable likeness, we are committed to a slide away from history into PSE and current affairs in which the past becomes information about origins. White's practical suggestion indicates a narrow conception of history as providing necessary information for personal and social functioning, at odds with the wider conception of history as a way of looking at the world, past and present, distant or recent, European or 'world', which has informed the best of recent practice. Other—historical—criteria lie behind this wider conception. Pupils need to understand long-term change, to grasp the differences between short and long-run importance, to see how different kinds of significance can be attributed to the same changes in different temporal and spatial contexts. They need to examine radically different ways of life from ours, and to understand alternative individual ideals. Some ideas may be best acquired in passages of the past very clearly not concerned with the issues people confront today: the distance allows judgement relatively untrammelled by assimilation to immediate prejudices. Of course recent history should be taught, and of course the Secretary of State put himself and the history curriculum in an absurd position by allowing history to be abandoned at 14, but White should not find odd, or dismiss with vague references to time-slicing, the possibility that Medieval Realms should occupy 'the same curricular space' as Britain in the 20th century.

White's complaint about the effect of government abandonment of history and geography to the status of optional subjects after 14 seems misplaced. The government's last-minute failure to stick to its own convictions in the face of headteachers' complaints that timetable changes imposed by the National Curriculum were unworkable can hardly be blamed on the Working Party or the NCC committee. A major source of pressure on timetables was headteachers' commitment to the view that personal and social aims should take priority over the expansion of understanding. This meant that history and geography has had to give way to PSE and TVEI-type courses where personal and social aims were thought to be *directly* addressed.[24]

All this underlines the importance of taking history into account—the history of history teaching—if we are not to misunderstand the issue confronting the Working Party, and to criticize unfairly both the Working Party and the NCC history committee. Many criticisms could be made of *History in the National Curriculum* and its earlier incarnations, but to accuse the Working Party or the NCC committee of mere chronological time-slicing is to miss what was at stake. The assumption that 'chronological time-slicing', whatever that may be, is the 'the conventional practice of history teachers' is wide of the mark for the same reason: it ignores the changes in history teaching over the last two decades which provoked the furore over history.

The reality is that the 'methodological aims intrinsic to the discipline' could not be 'taken as read', because they were at the root of the dispute about the 'new history'; behind the argument of those who questioned such aims was the idea that other—social—priorities should override them. The Working Party and the NCC committee succeeded in preserving the methodological aims in the face of very great pressure, and for this, at least, won the gratitude of many history teachers. History may survive to contribute to wider educational aims precisely because the Working Party and the NCC committee fended off attempts to saddle it with transient versions of social and personal aims at the expense of what makes it worthwhile as the rational study of the past.

NOTES

1 White J, 'The Purpose of School History: Has The National Curriculum Got It Right?', in this collection, (1992), p.18.

2 Lee, P. J., 'Historical Knowledge and the National Curriculum', in Aldrich, R (ed.) *History in the national Curriculum*, (Bedford Way series), London, Kogan Page, 1991, p.42.

3 Beattie, A., *History in Peril: may parents preserve it*, CPS, London, 1987, p.10 and passim.

4 Lee, (1991), p.43

5 Lee, (1991), p.42.

6 Lee, (1991), p.43

7   White, (1992), p.11, referring to Lee, P. J., 'Why Learn History', in Dickinson, A. K., Lee, P. J. and Rogers, P. J., (eds.), *Learning History*, Heinemann Educational Books, London, 1984, p.13. The passage in which this sentence is set is as follows: Some history may be better than none but how can history compete for time with other disciplines? After all, it is plainly not so useful as science or mathematics. The weakness of this objection is in its crude conception of what is useful. The useful is often set against the intrinsically valuable, and there is some sense in such a juxtaposition. But something that expands one's conception of the world does not fall exactly into either category. At the same time it would be odd to assert that whatever produced such an expansion is useless even if it is not applicable to a specific goal on the model of technology. It is often forgotten that the greatest achievements of science have been of this wider, non technological kind. Activities like this are valuable, both intrinsically and as means to ends.

8   White, (1992), p.11

9   White, (1992), p.14

10 'The Enlightenment's contribution to the formation of our national identity' does not get White out of this corner. Our national identity (which is not quite as homogeneous as the phrase suggests) is a result of many disparate contributions: the reason for valuing impartiality and objectivity in history is because without it there is no history, not that it is a product of one strand of one nation's history.

11 I agree with John White that the enabling role of history is extremely important: thinking historically may be a necessary condition of being a democratic citizen— under some descriptions of 'democratic citizen'. But this means that history contributes in an important way to educational aims, not that it can arrogate these to itself. (This relationship between aims of history and aims of education is pursued further below.)

12 White, (1992), p.14

13 All this is elaborated in the two papers to which White refers; there is no space to re-iterate the details here. For an attempt to unpack the aims of history, see Lee, (1991). For a discussion of the way in which history reaches beyond itself, see Lee, (1984).

14 White, (1992), p.18

15 White, (1992), p.15

16 White, (1992), ibid

17 Being aware of choices is not, of course, being good at making them. Suppose that investigation of the connection between being aware of choices and making them showed that too much awareness damaged practical autonomy of action (as opposed to a theoretical autonomy which is really neither more nor less than what is offered in the transformative aims of history and science)? If White refused to abandon the expansion of knowledge and understanding as an aim at that point, it would presumably be because he thought the transformations that expansion brings about are somehow important in themselves?

18   The difficulty with this kind of move is that, once history is harnessed directly to personal and social aims in this way—i.e. not through the transformative aim—it ceases to offer the benefits even of the transformative aim. Of course, if autonomy is interdefined with the expansion of historical understanding and the transformative aim, then the distinction between personal and social aims and aims to do with the expansion of understanding begins to blur.

19   White, (1992), p.16

20   White, (1992), p.15

21   But there may be a case for claiming that the activity of history itself presupposes at least a concern for freedom to assert what the evidence leads us to believe (for ourselves, and for others); and also a conception of man as rational (as opposed to irrational). (See Lee, (1991), endnote 21, p.16.) This presupposition might be extended to include equality of treatment of, and respect for, persons as sources of arguments. It is too much to claim that this adds up to an allegiance to liberal-democratic community, but there appears to be at least an overlap of interests.

22   I would agree, for example, with most of White's comments on p.17 of his paper about what pupils may gain from the study of history.

23   Some empirical evidence is available as to what is realistic in history. See the studies listed in Lee, (1991), note 12; and also Shemilt, D. J., *History 13-16: Evaluation Study*, Holmes McDougall, Edinburgh, 1981.

24   Some schools organized timetables which met the original National Curriculum criteria without much difficulty: there was no real practical need to make foundation subjects optional.

HISTORY AND LOVE OF THE PAST

Paddy Walsh

The two most frequently mentioned motives for the study of history are the love of the past, or 'history for its own sake', and the desire to understand the present in the light of its past. I shall argue that the first of these, taken in its plainest and strongest sense, should be given priority over the second, in effect that history should be approached as primarily a form of ancestor-communing (while taking a wide view of who our ancestors are).

The meaning of love of the past

'Love of the past' is sometimes interpreted as love of enquiry into the past.[1] The rigid detachment favoured in some academic circles lends itself to this interpretation: if the historian may not engage humanly and ethically with her subjects what backward-looking motive remains but the enjoyment of the play of intelligence and imagination in reconstructing a piece of history? But since 'puzzle-solving' hardly captures that importance we feel history to possess, the way is then clear to making its contemporary relevance the main public and educational point of history.

Peter Lee has interestingly suggested that 'history for its own sake' can be more substantially interpreted in terms of history being not just another means by which we may achieve our present ends, but something which expands our whole picture of the world and of human beings, and, therefore, of what ends are possible for us.[2] But is even this strong enough? It actually risks seeing history as a means to the 'second-order' end of reconsidering our ends in life. More fundamentally, it raises the question of whether it is a condition of history opening up new ends for us that we approach the people of the past, not just as important learning resources, but as *ends-in-themselves*. Is it a matter only of the objectivity that respects evidence and the limits of evidence, seeks to get the account right, and resists capture in advance by particular practical ends and interests in the present? Or is it a matter of a deeper objectivity that seeks also to 'do justice' to the past?

35

There is such a thing as a brotherly and sisterly love directed to the human beings and the human worlds that are dead and gone, or at any rate to some of them—'piety' in its old meaning—and this indeed is the plainest interpretation of 'love of the past'. There is nothing the least bit necrophilic about such love. Past figures, deeds, institutions and movements more or less spontaneously engage our attention, respect, admiration, compassion, indignation, sense of justice, and so forth, and we tend naturally to justify such responses by essentially the same considerations we would use in regard to the contemporary world. Whatever the differences in coming to the relevant factual judgements in the two cases, once the judgements are in they spontaneously evoke or command the same range of feelings, values and attitudes, and that the contemporary 'now' has a dramatic and ethical edge over the historical 'then' affects the strength rather than the nature of these responses. What good reason could we have to block such responses to the past, unless it be the kind of reason that could also be relevant in regard to the present—that they are in the particular case inappropriate, hasty, partial, and unjust?

Yet explicit acknowledgements of this 'human' involvement with history are extremely hard to find. Thus the Final Report of the National Curriculum History Working Group suggests no fewer than nine purposes of school history[3], of which only one, 'to arouse interest in the past', even gestures at 'piety'. Considering the obligations of such a Group to consult the way historians actually work, we may assume that piety is not a prominent part of the self-image of history as a discipline.

A part of the explanation of this is the general influence of positivism in the human sciences—it tends to depersonalize the scientist/subject relationship. But we must consider a more particular objection to a 'human' involvement with the subjects of research when those subjects are dead and gone. This is that we cannot relate *reciprocally* to the past (as we can to the present). We cannot shape and influence it nor, therefore, take responsibility for it. Let us comment on this in two stages. First, the obvious kernel of truth in it does not render love of the past inappropriate. Many of our responses to present human beings do not require the setting of a reciprocal relationship, nor do they all seek a practical expression in actions performed in or around the person responded to. Admiration, for instance, can be anonymous, and is not immediately practical. But even in the case of responses like compassion or indignation that do carry a fairly immediate complement of appropriate actions, practical helplessness is frustrating without making the compassion or indignation itself inappropriate. The helpless victim of torture still has the right to her indignation. So does the helpless observer of it. So, too, will the future historian of it.

Second, we are not *entirely* helpless in regard to the past. One thing we can do for it is set the record straight posthumously—reinstate the stoned prophets. Certainly this is a far from easy business—particularly where time has not yielded the oppressed their revenge in the form of ultimate victory or emancipation. Simone Weil wrote in 1939 that if the Nazis were to win the coming war the historians of two thousand years hence might still be lauding the 'Pax Germanica'![4] Yet she thought it possible, and a sacred duty, to begin to reconstruct and vindicate civilizations like the Trojan, Carthaginian, Celtic, Inca and American Indian—by a huge effort of attention and imagination in regard to such scraps of them as have survived—and herself contributed to such an effort in regard to the 11th century civilization of Languedoc.[5]

We can also allow the light of the past to inform the way we live our lives. This is much more than 'conserving the legacy' of the past, there being quick distinctions to remind ourselves of between the mummification and the use of the past, and between tradition as a dead weight and tradition as a source of strength and inspiration.[6] We may also distinguish the more general light that history is admitted, perhaps even by academic historians, to cast on the human predicament, e.g. the tendency for victorious might to assume the mantle of right, from the more specific lessons and inspirations that we can take from particular bits of history, e.g. a greater devotion to democratic institutions, scientific freedom, the cause of feminism, a particular trade-union, or a church. Now when we consciously and critically take aboard some specific lesson from a part of history, when our awareness and devotion relating to some cause or value are intensified by a study of the labour, pain and hope that have gone into it, then another mode of piety is at work. We are, and we see ourselves to be, in fraternal and sororal cooperation with some individuals and groups of the past—and in opposition to others.

Someone will insist that such 'cooperation' with the past remains a kind of fiction, since for all our efforts to live by the best of it we still cannot change one jot in it. But that objection forgets something: the past would have been very different if its individuals and peoples had never worked with an eye to a *future beyond themselves*, never participated in designs which they knew would not be realised in their lifetimes in the faith that others would be encouraged to carry the venture forward. 'Partnership with the past' has the same validity, in fact, as 'partnership with the future' and 'why worry about the past—we can do nothing for it?' is as cynical as 'what has posterity ever done for me?'

The primacy of love of the past

So far we have been working on the substantial sense and validity of 'love of the human past'. What now of its proposed priority in relation to the other main motive for doing history? The idea to ponder here is that only those who love the past for itself can be trusted to mediate it to the present, to draw the *right* lessons from it and indicate its *proper* relevance—and they are precisely those who will not regard such lessons and relevance as the *ground*-motive of their concern with the past.

In effect, this idea draws an analogy from our relationships in the present. We distinguish personal relationships from those that are simply cooperative or contractual. In authentic friendship, love, or even colleagueship, we value the other for himself or herself. The common ventures, exchanges of benefits, and lessons learnt are 'spin-off', and they have a value as expressions, symbols and nourishments of the relationship as well as their own utility. Note, however, that their utility is not generally less significant for being indirect. The paradox is, indeed, that there are certain highly important kinds of benefit—for instance, in the area of self-knowledge and self-valuation—which can *only* be acquired in relationships in which they are not the primary focus of attention. If someone conducts a personal relationship for the primary purpose of learning from it, perhaps to gain 'experience' in such relationships, we say he is 'using' the other person—but, more to the point, we suspect such a relationship defeats its own purpose and yields a lower dividend in terms of learning and experience. Does a similar logic obtain in historical study?

Among our relationships with past individuals, institutions, movements, cultures and societies, many come to resemble more 'the personal' than 'the useful'—is that not why we locate history among 'the humanities'? We may expect then that among the lessons which the past has for us some important ones will be ours only if we enter into such quasi-personal relationships with it and are authentic about this, i.e. do not have these lessons as our direct and primary object. And surely this is in fact so. No doubt we can, without thus involving ourselves, 'strip-mine' the past quite effectively for many of its deposits. We have the beginnings of an idea in philosophy, for instance, and we search the works of past thinkers on the subject for helpful developments of it. We can also keep this 'using' within moral bounds by observing the minimal conventions of respect, acknowledging our sources, avoiding misrepresentation, and so on. But we could not mine in this way some more precious things: some steady insight into human heads and hearts, an abiding sense of the fragility of a certain value, a new vitality in some important project—in general, the contribution of history to wisdom and care. For that an altogether more serious commitment to the past seems necessary.

Pre-critical and critical history

It will be objected that this position does away with 'critical history', that 'piety' is exactly what was characteristic of pre-critical history. Now I doubt if there is any wholly agreed account of the distinction between critical and pre-critical history, but let us work with the following fairly typical set of contrasts: precritical history is a) ethnocentric, b) practical and c) ethical; whereas critical history is a.) universal, b) explanatory and c) non-judgemental, even value-free.[7] Considering each of these three contrasts in relation to our support for 'piety' will also help us clarify that notion further.

a) Pre-critical history is largely confined, it is said, to the history of one's own community or society, and where it reaches out to other societies it considers them only in their relevance to one's own. Critical history is universal in its intended scope, and when it addresses itself to other societies it endeavours to do so on their own terms. It may even prefer to work on societies and times that are particularly remote from the historian's own.

This contrast forces us to a vital clarification: there is no need to conceive 'piety' as a duty only to one's own forbears—that would be moral childishness. In fact, the logic of piety replicates the logic of charity. There is an important sense in which each is to be universal—as 'openness' to all rather than as (impossible) realization. On the other hand, piety and charity 'begin at home', both in the sense that they must first be learnt there, and in the sense that unless one goes on loving one's own that is near at hand one's protestations regarding what is distant become suspect. There are also grounds other than kinship on which actual charity becomes obligatory or specially desirable, and to each of these also there is an analogue for piety. In both there are the special claims upon us of the afflicted and oppressed, of our own urgent needs—in particular as viewed morally and spiritually, of those we have already engaged and become friendly with, and of those that circumstances have just now put squarely in our way. Thus an historian or a student might, in piety, work on a period or society because it had been neglected by other historians especially if its people had been oppressed and destroyed, or because it possessed virtues that she believed she and her times stood in special need of, or because she was an authority on it and therefore responsible for it, or because she felt a spontaneous affinity with it, or because a school or university syllabus is forcing it on her. Piety, then, requires no return to a pre-critical ethnocentrism. On the other hand, neither does it accord with the flat and *a priori* neutrality of the first proposed canon of critical history. It has criteria for judging and assigning priorities, though ones that are broad and generous.

b) Pre-critical history, like the folk-memory from which it evolves, is said to have an overriding *practical* function, namely, to promote the society's sense of its own identity and its devotion to its own survival and development. It tells the stories of the society's existing institutions (or perhaps of revolutionary ones being struggled for), contrasts these favourably with those of other societies, refutes the 'calumnies' of neighbours regarding them, and legitimates the power-structure embodied in them. Its effectiveness for these ends sometimes requires of it a consummate artistry. Critical history, however, is (or was) said to have no practical function, and to regard political and apologetic aims as fatal to the achievement of its task. That task is simply to discover what was really going forward at a particular place and time, and why, and to set this forth in a significant narrative—preferably in plain prose. So, its explanatory drive is directed not at the present, but at the past itself and it proceeds by a greater and greater concentration on the detail of the past, and an ever more thorough discarding of the historian's contemporary reflexes and presuppositions in favour of an imaginative assumption of those of the times he is studying.[8]

How does 'piety' stand in relation to this purported contrast? First, and again like charity, piety has critical as well as appreciative modes: it may express itself very well in bitter condemnation of things done by one's country or one's forbears. Second, this account of pre-critical history generalises unjustly. Folk-history has been known to beat its breast rather than justify itself at all costs, to acknowledge some of the people's past crimes rather than glorify them. The Old Testament occasionally achieved this moral objectivity and the Iliad's sorrowful evocation of the tyranny of war over both victor and vanquished is a remarkable example of it.[9] Third, the polarization in the stated contrast between practical relevance on the one hand, and the past for its own sake on the other hand, is extreme. Our argument has been that these are organically related: if (but only if) the past is explored for its own sake, its more profound relevance to the present may be realised.

c) Finally, it is said, pre-critical history is *ethical.* As well as narrating, it apportions praise and blame. It is a tribunal before which people and deeds of the past pass in review to be condemned, or excused, or commended. But the critical historian professes to eschew ethical judgement and he is severe on those historians who indulge in it. Thus Butterfield condemned Lord Acton and those he called generally 'Whig historians' in a classic essay. In part this was for the arrogance implicit in their wholesale judgements of others. But in addition Butterfield believed that the intrusion of moral judgement in historical enquiry led to a loss of objectivity in the work.

It is not clear that moral indignation is not a dispersion of one's energies to the great confusion of one's judgement.[10]

It tended, if not quite to a falsification of the historical details, at any rate to premature and artificial synopses of broad historical developments, based on a simplistic division of historical agents and ideas into 'good' and 'bad', 'progressive' and 'reactionary', or—in other hands—'loyal' and 'subversive'. This issue seems the most critical for our recommendation of piety.

We might note, first, that piety (like charity) is not all ethical encounter. It is also fascination with the past, enjoyment of it, aesthetic delight at it, polite tolerance of occasional boredom with it, and so on. Furthermore, insofar as it is ethical, piety is essentially independent both of an a priori belief in historical progress (such as was held by the 'Whig' historians) and of the romanticisation of the past. It implies no case, not even a *prima facie* one, for placing the present (and its historians) on a moral eminence in relation to the past—or the reverse. In advance of a particular study, the probability-values should be equal of the historian and the present being put in ethical question, and of the past to be studied being put in question. This is indeed to expect impartiality from the historian, but an impartiality that differs from, and goes deeper than, ethical neutrality. Again, while it is obvious that certain kinds of moral fervour would distort historical accounts, the claim that moral interest *necessarily* distorts assumes that a self-critical moral objectivity is an impossible, maybe incoherent, ideal. If

41

it is only very difficult then one could, perhaps, convict academic history of a failure of nerve: history is made easier at the price of making it less significant.

It might be replied that, at any rate in an age of moral pluralism like ours, history as a cooperative venture requires a *methodological* exclusion of value- judgements. And, after all, if professional historians can only get the bald narrative together the readers or audience can still, if they wish, use it towards their own personal 'ethical encounters' with the past.[11] There may be *something* in this suggestion. In a pluralist society history-writing might be better for taking account of the pluralism of contemporary values, laying special emphasis on the values that are shared, being explicit about relevant more 'personal' values, and so forth—in other words, for adopting the manners and procedures of everyday ethical discourse in this kind of society. Again, there may be some useful distinction to be drawn between the actual moment of historical enquiry, to which the Weberian 'value-relevant but value-free' adage would apply, and our wider and more general relationship with the fruits of that enquiry. But even if this distinction could be made completely firm, a proper historical involvement—and education—would still have to include both.

The non-neutrality of perspective

But the deeper question raised by this last exchange is of the very *possibility* of ethical neutrality in an historical narrative retaining at least some human significance. And this is the moment to acknowledge that our account of critical history is one that would have appealed more a generation ago. Today's historian is more likely to be sceptical about the possibility of value-free history. In particular, the overall organization or *perspective* of a work is now commonly seen as influenced (at least) by factors which the historian has brought to her enquiry from outside history. Perspectives can differ without conflicting, as would the histories of the science and the art of the same period, or they may conflict, as would socialist and non-socialist accounts of the industrial revolution. The sheer bulk and diversity of the materials of history guarantee an endless supply of perspectives in the first sense. Now even this point presents some difficulty for the old-style critical faith that, in Bury's words, 'a complete assemblage of the smallest facts of human history will tell in the end'.[12] It does not seem reconcilable with the atomism of that ideal, suggesting, rather, that 'facts' are only intelligible, and only noticed, in some degree of relationship to perspectives formed or being formed. But the difficulty is clearer in conflicts of perspective. Here the governing differences (that are not, or not in all respects, to be resolved by further historical research and discovery) are not just matters of the historian's personal interests, but of her metaphysical and moral beliefs. The crucial point is that these beliefs and attitudes participate *inevitably* in the shaping of an historical enquiry.

We may broadly distinguish two respects in which they do. First the historian's views of *what is possible*, whether in nature as it impinges on people or for human nature itself—will be more or less remote operators of the interpretation she puts on historical data. They inevitably affect her attitude to testimonies and other sources, limit the hypotheses she is prepared to entertain, and so on. One may say that if these views are right it is perfectly proper that they should do these things. But the question of their rightness is not an historical question, not at any rate an exclusively historical question. The point is at least as old as Hume's reflections on the historian's attitude to miracles.[13] One should be careful, however, not to overstate it. There is no good reason for assuming that historical study itself makes no contribution to our views on what is possible. On the contrary, this might well be thought one of its more important values. But though the historical evidence may suggest reappraisal of our views of the possible, it will not by itself *determine* them.

Second, there is the inevitable influence of the historian's broad moral outlook— that is, of her view of *what is humanly important*. We can see this through a distinction between the *intrinsic* and the *instrumental* importance of an historical event. Instrumentally, an event's importance is measured by the extent of its causal influence on other events (the loss of a horse-shoe nail may bring the kingdom down). Intrinsically, its importance is independent of anything that happens afterwards. If one claimed the French Revolution was the most important event in modern history, one might well have both kinds of importance in mind. Again, if history has shifted its focus from the doings of kings and queens to the common person, it is likely that this reflects both a post-Marx perception of economic and associated social movements as more *influential* than the actions of monarchs, and our *ethical* beliefs about the rights of people and the value of democracy. So, history may be structured by moral values even if it eschews overt moral judgement.[14] But we can surely go further and claim that it must be so structured. For instrumental importance must itself depend on intrinsic importance. Every event has, perhaps, an infinitude of ripples. So the significance, as well as the quantity, of actual consequences must be involved in judging instrumental importance, and that means that intrinsic importance, and at any rate broad values, are always involved in historical selection and construction.

We have found reason to doubt some standard contrasts between pre-critical and critical history. In the end it may be that the only real differences between them are that a properly conceived critical history is more concerned constantly to expand the story of the past, more concerned with getting the story right, and is methodologically better equipped to achieve that expansion and that fidelity. And those differences, though this is not how it is usually put, could themselves be conceived as developments in piety, expressions of a greater piety!

NOTES

1   An influential and well known work that does this is W. H. Walsh (1967. 3rd revised edition).
2   Lee 1991 pp. 42-3
3   The nine are: to help understand the present in the context of the past; to arouse interest in the past; to help to give pupils a sense of identity; to help to give pupils an understanding of their own cultural roots and shared inheritances; to contribute to pupils' knowledge and understanding of other countries and other cultures in the modern world; to train the mind by means of disciplined study; to introduce pupils to the distinctive methodology of historians; to enrich other areas of the curriculum; and to prepare pupils for adult life. National Curriculum History Working Group Report 1990, paragraph 1.7.
4   'The Great Beast. Some reflections on the origins of Hitlerism' in Weil, (1962).
5   See 'A medieval epic poem' and 'The Romanesque Renaissance' in *ibid.*
6   See Nietzsche's essay on *The Use and Abuse of History*.
7   These points of contrast are borrowed from Lonergan (1972), pp. 185 ff. Chs. 6-10 of this distinguished theological study offer an extremely useful survey and analysis of issues relating to the study of history. Note that theology, because of the combination of historical with philosophical and experiential claims that an historical religion involves, has been to the forefront in considering these matters.
8   Lonergan *ibid.*
9   See Simone Weil's brilliant essay 'The Iliad, A Poem of Force'.
10   Butterfield, (1931)
11   Or, it might be recommended that comparative ethics be held over and approached systematically in a discipline distinct from history proper, to be called 'dialectics' perhaps, for which history would provide the data, as Lonergan recommends, *supra cit.*—in this, I think, echoing Schleiermacher.
12   Bury, J. B., 'The Science of History', reprinted in Bury (1927)
13   *Essay Concerning Human Understanding*
14   I have borrowed both this distinction and these examples from Walsh, W. H., *supra cit.* Appendix A. 'The Limits of Scientific History' (3rd revised edition only).

WHERE THERE IS DOGMA, LET US SOW DOUBT

John Slater

I shall declare two sets of assumptions: first about what history is; later about what a liberal-democratic community is. Then, as my colleagues have done, I want to explore what the connection between the two might be. Let me say, at the outset, that I find Peter Lee's statement that 'history has no necessary connection with a democratic perspective' (p. 27) a touch too dismissive, while John White's belief that 'the main reason for teaching history in schools is as a necessary element in the cultivation of those personal qualities of students...which fit them to be citizens of a liberal democratic society' (p. 20) is more than a touch prescriptive. Paddy Walsh's concept of 'piety' may help us reconcile, perhaps not inappropriately, these two points of view.

History is what people have recorded about the past. It is less than all the past, but considerably more than what is remembered. It is simultaneously and essentially a way of investigating the past and of authenticating statements about it. The central substantive content preoccupation of history is the evidence of the behaviour of identifiable human beings as it changes through time. Not all human beings throughout the whole of time can be studied. Historians are obliged to select. Selection involves a value-judgement which gives public importance and status to those who are selected and implicitly, sometimes deliberately, denies it to those who are not. History is not a value-free enterprise. All these characteristics justify the status of history as a distinct subject and discipline.

There are two further characteristics of history which set it apart, in emphasis at least, from some other disciplines. First, its pedagogical aims cannot easily be defined in terms of precise destinations, completed tasks, and problems to be solved. (I always twitch uneasily when I see 'problem solving' as an aim in a history scheme of work.) History does not allow us to say 'Ah, now I know all about the Civil War', 'Now I understand exactly why there was a war in Vietnam, or why Auschwitz existed'. Outcomes of studying history are unpredictable, often unexpected and generally modest—a matter of diminishing ignorance and lessening misunderstanding. There remains, however, always the exciting possibility that there is perhaps more still to discover.

Second, history presents its students with simple, sometimes beguilingly accessible, images and ideas: tidy explanations; right and wrong, quite distinct and easily recognised; conveniently enumerated causes and consequences. Good Queen Bess and Bloody Mary, the 'free world', terrorists or freedom fighters, six causes of the Great War: images often perpetuated and confirmed by textbooks and examination papers. More often are they part of our inherited culture and traditions, the attitudes of families and peer groups, comics and the media. But historical thinking obliges us to recognise the subtleties, complexities and contradictions which lurk behind the myths with which we often live. The enemy of such thinking is the stereotype and dogma.

History establishes the status of doubt. Paddy Walsh sees doubt not only as 'challenging simple moral categories', but also as a crucial characteristic of 'piety'. Well, if so, I am happy, in this sense at least, to be pious.

This is what history *is*. But what exactly is history *for*? And for whom? These questions are not primarily pedagogical; they are partly political and fundamentally philosophical. I am not a philosopher and oscillate between regretting this lack and doubtfully observing the emperor in his new clothes. I am grateful to my three colleagues for their essays which attempt to answer these questions with an illuminating combination, touched in all three essays by vision, of philosophical insights and dogged questioning. I was constantly stimulated and provoked, sometimes baffled, occasionally irritated. Nevertheless, they powerfully persuade me that teacher training has perhaps surrendered too easily to accusations of imbalance in favour of theoretical study. Without a philosophical foundation we cannot claim to be training future professionals. Without it teachers will find it difficult to understand the function of their teaching, add conviction to their expertise and be able to identify and resist the threats to it.

Running through all three essays are a series of distinctions and contrasts. Some are unhelpful (between 'history for its own sake' and 'instrumentalism'), others are misleading or confusing ('intrinsic' and 'extrinsic', 'reason' and 'aim'), or absent ('intention' and 'consequence') or illuminating ('historical aims' and 'educational aims').

It was once suggested that Her Majesty's Inspectorate should try to write about the curriculum for a year without using the terms 'breadth', 'depth', 'balance', 'coherence'. Close students of HMI writing will realise that the suggestion was not taken up. Indeed these terms still continue to muddy the language of the National Curriculum. They are all metaphors. So, too, is the phrase 'history for its own sake'. We would be the better for abandoning it. Who is the 'it' on whose behalf history is learnt? Someone other than the learner or the historian? Clio perhaps? Alas, she does not exist. Neither does her virginity, or the need to protect it from the harsh threats of instrumentalism. Studying 'history for its own sake' has become a slogan used by the educational right wing, striving to divert students of history away from uncomfortable critical skills which question and challenge assumptions rather than transmit values. On the other hand history which internalises its aims—is studied 'for its own sake'—is seen as a protection against instrumentalism, a nasty market economy and unworthy wealth-acquiring activities. Suspicion of 'instrumentalism' has always been just a little defensive and prim.

Let us also abandon the polarity which has been set up between 'internalised' or 'intrinsic' aims. 'Polarity' is, I suppose, another metaphor misleadingly suggesting an antithesis, alternatives, the need to choose. 'Continuum' is a better word. 'Spectrum' a preferred metaphor. At one end there is, say, the retired, financially independent scholar studying history, not for 'its' sake but, happily and indulgently, for his or hers. Further along the spectrum is John White's university scholar, immersing herself in the Anglo-Saxon penal system but perhaps not unaware of the esteem, or envy, of her fellow medievalists, or the stipend and fellowship justified by her scholarship. Next to her, and perhaps more publicly instrumental, is a PGCE student with his history degree, continuing with its study in order to find employment in a school. Finally, there is the young A-level history student being interviewed for a post in industry or business and quoting the words of an employer:

The study of English or history teaches not only the object of the discipline but also the method. The object may subsequently be discarded, dates and kings forgotten, but the methods by which they learnt remain and provide the means to acquire new information and expertise...A general arts and humanities education provides the young school leaver with the ability to adapt to a range of work demands. It makes them more employable than technologists with a single highly perishable skill. The need to equip young school leavers in the job market should be reflected in widening their options, not narrowing them. (Andrew Cowie, an employer, in the *Observer*, 24 January 1988)

All four love history. None has undermined its integrity. All have used it, in some part, for ends outside and beyond history; some have studied it with that intention. All are instrumentalists. None has, as Paddy Walsh suggested they should, felt obliged to prioritise their aims. They, as John White urges, 'uncoercedly chose their route', if not through history, certainly with it. Choice is, arguably, central to a liberal-democratic community.

What characterises a liberal-democratic community? It is pluralist as it contains groups and individuals who may be, for example, culturally, spiritually, politically, economically diverse. Inevitably there will be men and women, young and old. Second, and crucially, it is an open community. A pluralist community is not necessarily open. Hitler's Germany, even more Stalin's Soviet Russia, were pluralist as South Africa has always been. An open society does not see diversity as aberrant. Minimally, diversity is accepted as inevitable. Ideally, it is seen as a quality not a problem. But for a society or a nation to be liberal-democratic it is not enough to leave it to the aspirations and attitudes of individuals. Liberal democracy has to be institutionalised, for example, in parliaments and elections, the recognition of a free press, of trades unions, of the right to worship, and so on. The core question is 'what happens when there is disagreement?' A liberal-democratic society seeks *publicity* to involve all parties in resolving the dispute; it guarantees that all parties will survive the resolution; it ensures that the outcome can always be changed. Liberal democracy is not Utopian. None ever gets all that is wanted. Its continuity depends on compromises and second bests. Its qualities are negative. It is a vision tempered by deals. The learning of history in such a society benefits from its openness but is not exempt from its limitations.

Peter Lee's 'transformed' pupils will have learnt within such a society and inescapably been affected by it. Learning history could well change and enable them, for example, through holidays, reading, museum and gallery visits, to have entered into a lifelong affectionate relationship with the past, or to have become a teacher, or a more informed voter, or a tedious saloon-bar, barrack-room lawyer—all with noticeable impact on the society of his or her family, the school or the pub. Or they could have reacted strongly against a diet of learning facts about famous dead people and become computer programmers, estate agents or bouncers. All were consequences but they were not aims; none could be predicted, some not even anticipated. It was not the role of history either to set the agenda or to prioritise it. Transformative aims are neither extrinsic or intrinsic. Both could be consequences. Neither can be goals.

Now John White is worried that Lee appears to favour his 'transformative aim' over others such as the promotion of patriotism or good citizenship. I am unhappy with these concepts, particularly 'good citizenship'; there is considerable public debate in this country on whether we are 'citizens' or 'subjects', whether we ought to be one rather than the other, and just what the terms mean anyway. History can help us understand the debate, not pre-empt its outcome. There is also a problem in the use, not of the word 'transformative', but of 'aim', which unhelpfully distinguishes between 'process' and 'goal' (another misleading metaphor!). 'Transformation', like Walsh's 'openness to all' is not an outcome but an integral part of learning history—concurrent, not subsequent. Favouring good citizenship over transformation is not really a question that arises; the two concepts are quite different. Perhaps the confusion has been increased by a shift of terminology. Lee originally claimed that changing pupils was a *reason* for teaching history, not an aim. 'Transformation' is a part of the enabling process; good citizenship is merely one example of what conceivably might be enabled.

Some outcomes may be valuable but in no way dependent on history, for example, the application of critical and analytical skills to management training. Others may more closely relate to learning history, such as being a more informed citizen, while other outcomes may have history as a necessary if not always a sufficient condition: understanding the historical context and roots of a culture or community, working in a museum or becoming a history teacher. The integrity of history is threatened if these outcomes are prioritised by the learning. History does not prioritise. *People* prioritise.

John White sensibly, in my view, finds the 'intrinsic'/'extrinsic' distinction unhelpful, but fails to distinguish between the 'enabling' and 'guaranteeing' functions of history. In a key passage (White, p. 17) a number of statements related to the aims of history are made about British contemporary society: 'a major social framework for our lives is provided by *our* national community...*common* ties, including *shared* mores, a *shared* history and, to some extent, a *shared* language' (my italic). Well, maybe. These are value-laden assumptions. They are *not* assumptions to be transmitted. That is not a task for history. They are hypotheses to be tested, which is. The passage is not only confident about just what is shared in our society, but prescriptive about the action we must take: 'children *need* to be brought up with a certain degree of attachment to this larger polity...They *must* see themselves bound to other members of the community.' One of the characteristics of the liberal-democratic community which all four authors patently believe in is that education enables *choice* between genuine alternatives and does not seek to guarantee any one of them. This is recognised in the National Curriculum in Attainment Target 2 (Interpretations of History) and in the significant pluralism of the History Working Group's references to 'heritages'. I find it difficult to reconcile White's view with his earlier statement which I applaud: 'One aspect of being an autonomous, i.e. self-directed, person in the conduct of one's life is that one uncoercedly chooses one's route through life' (White, p. 16). As Peter Lee writes (p. 29): 'History has no allegiance to liberal-democratic community as an ideal. It is concerned to explore communities of every kind, both in their own terms and in ours, where ours is *never to be taken as a single fixed perspective*' (my italic). And yet... Lee's changed pupils, as he describes, and our relationship with the past redefined and changed by Paddy Walsh's concept of piety, are unlikely to have flourished in a closed or authoritarian society. At the very least, the changed, pious, uncoerced pupil is a *symptom* of an open community. 'History' may have no allegiance to a liberal-democratic community, but a modest touch of gratitude from historians might not be out of place. A transformed pupil is an empowered pupil *and* an empowered member of that community, will modestly and perhaps barely perceptibly have changed it. Not an aim perhaps, but an outcome.

If some of the consequences of good history teaching, even if not always predictable, can easily be anticipated, why not accept them as an aim, for example, 'to enable more effective participation in a liberal-democratic society'? Here Lee's distinction between historical and educational aims is crucial. Historical aims are intrinsic to the subject, for example knowing and understanding about the legacy of the Roman Empire, or the impact on British society of the First World War; understanding and using historical terms such as BC and AD or 'feudalism'; understanding that historical statements are dependent on the critical evaluation of evidence, and so on. Educational aims are wider and do not depend on history, but are not separate from it. This may help us define what history is *for*, as opposed to what history must inevitably *be*: to help pupils better understand the world they live in, or their national, local and cultural roots, or be more informed voters. These wider educational aims can not only help us decide what history is for, they can also help identify criteria for selecting its content. John White is right to be suspicious that, if one of the functions of education is to help young people understand the contemporary world, it is unlikely to be effective if the history component is unbalanced in favour of the distant compared with the recent past. Origins are not a substitute for the present. Contemplating an acorn is no substitute for the shade of an oak tree.

In 1985 HMI published *History in the Primary and Secondary Years: an HMI view* (DES, 1985). It argued against a centrally prescribed curriculum content, but for some consensus on criteria for its selection. It argued against a centrally prescribed curriculum content, but for some consensus on criteria for its selection. One of these was 'an understanding of contemporary society' and suggested some issues to be borne in mind when selecting content: urban growth and demographic changes, the effect on our lives of science and technology, open societies which present young people with a range of social, political and moral choices, the changing status of women, a multicultural society and internationally interdependent society. These criteria were not historical, although at the time many of us thought they were. They were, in the broadest non-partisan sense, political, moral and educational. They were also value judgements based on the evidence of the recent past and a fair measure of anticipatory hunch.

If we distinguish between aims and consequences, how responsible are historians for them? The saloon-bar, barrack-room lawyer is, in part, one consequence of someone's teaching history. But it was never its aim. So *no* responsibility? Clearly some. But in general what is the balance of credit and blame? Three questions need to be addressed. They are concerned with (a) the level of children's understanding, (b) the openness of the historians' agenda and (c) the effects of historical thinking.

First, as history is concerned with provisional and tentative statements, with problems that have no solutions, questions with more than one answer, with establishing doubt, are we not seriously underestimating the need for clarity and predictability, particularly in the learning of young children? I cannot give a confident answer except to say that the evidence of HMI suggests that it is not a problem, provided, that is, the teachers are aware of the question. It may well be that it is less an issue of age or intelligence than of temperament. There are adults as well as children who are drawn more to predictability, precision and problem solving; others, to ambiguity, puzzles and mysteries. The task is not to exempt either group from ways of thinking they do not find easy, but to encourage their access to them.

Second, how open is the historians' agenda? After all, the aim is to enable pupils to make choices from *their* agenda. But is there perhaps a concealed agenda restricting choice? A history teacher would be gratified if an ex-pupil told her that her lessons had helped him gain a university place, or develop an enthusiasm for

51

local history or genealogy, given him insight into his local and cultural roots or become a more confident trades unionist. But a more informed and effective member of the National Front? A more confident racist? Is it reasonable not to feel gratified? Is history after all in the business of selecting out life options? If so, by what criteria? I believe there are two.

The first is historical. I have space to do little more than assert it. Prejudice and racial stereotyping are inconsistent with the historians' insistence that statements about individuals, groups or whole cultures must be consistent with available evidence. There is no evidential base for racism. This is no more negotiable than 12x12=144. We cannot prevent our pupils becoming members of the National Front. We cannot allow history to be used as their justification.

But there is another lurking doubt here. Are we not becoming judges rather than recorders of the past? Paddy Walsh reminds us of Butterfield's strictures on historians as judges. In *The Politics of History Teaching* (Slater, 1989, p. 11) I express some reservations:

> Herbert Butterfield was suspicious of historians making judgements. 'I don't think passing judgements is in the province of technical historians,' he said, 'I think that is God's job, that is God's history.' Only Gods can judge? I wonder. Surely only the Gods can be spectators?

Walsh also reminds us 'of the inescapable subjectivity with which we view the past'. Indeed. It cannot be the task of history to purge us of our subjective reactions, but to remind us of their existence and help us to hold them with a greater degree of knowledge and understanding. A balanced view of genocide would surely be impiety.

There are also sound educational criteria for limiting the agenda. We are all concerned with pupils in *schools*. Their function is to enable learning. They must strive to be havens. They will fail if any of their learners feel under-valued or threatened. A school fails, contradicts its function, if it seems to endorse, even indirectly, prejudice and discrimination. The liberal agenda is not boundless.

The third question concerns the aims and consequences of historical thinking. It is proper to ask how societies can survive without decisions being taken and problems solved, if confidence is eroded with doubt, if the need to judge is blunted by a compassionate awareness of alternatives and contexts—all encouraged by history. But historical thinking is only one strand of thinking. History is rational, demands evidence, and accepts alternative interpretations based on it. On the other hand political thinking, for example, as opposed to political education, is concerned with the organisation and public assertion of one partial point of view. Government and its civil servants *have* to take decisions, usually without having solved the problems. Religious belief is not authenticated but evidence in the historical sense, nor is the love between two people, nor the emotional impact of landscape or great art; mathematics and science demand a far greater measure of predictability. Constitutionally a liberal-democratic society is characterised by a separation and a *balance* of powers. None dominates, all contribute. So it is with patterns of thinking. Historical thinking does not claim priority, but without it pupils will be disabled. It is part of a balanced curriculum better defined, not by what subjects are called, but by what they do and are for. Historical thinking provides procedural conditions for making statements about other human beings. Its enemies are stereotypes and dogma. Doubt is our weapon—at least I think so.

REFERENCES

Anderson, B. (1983) *Imagined Communities: reflections on the origin and spread of nationalism.* London: Verso.

Beattie, A. (1987) *History in Peril: may parents preserve it.* London: Centre for Policy Studies, p 10 and passim.

Bury, J. B. (1927) 'The science of history', in Tempereley, H. (1930), *Selected Essays, J.B. Bury,*

Butterfield, H. (1931) *The Whig Interpretation of History.* London: Bell.

Department of Education and Science (DES) (1985) *History in the Primary and Secondary Years: an HMI view.* London: HMSO.

Department of Education and Science (DES) (1989) *National Curriculum History Working Group: Interim Report.*

Department of Education and Science (DES) (1990) *National Curriculum History Working Group: Final Report.*

Education Reform Act, 1988 London: HMSO.

Hume, D. (1777 ed., pub 1975) *Essays Concerning Human Understanding.* Oxford: Clarendon Press.

Lee, P. (1984) 'Why learn history?' in A Dickinson *et al. Learning History.* London: Heinemann.

Lee, P. (1991) 'Historical knowledge and the National Curriculum' in Aldrich, R., (ed) *History in the National Curriculum.* London: Kogan Page in association with the Institute of Education, University of London.

Lonergan, B. (1972) *Method in Theology.* London: Darton, Longman and Todd.

Miller, D. (1988) 'The ethical significance of nationality' *Ethics 98.*

Nietzsche, F. W. (tr. 1949, 1957) *The Use and Abuse of History.* New York: Bobbs-Merrill, Library of Liberal Arts.

Shemilt, D. J. (1981) *History 13-16: evaluation study.* Edinburgh: Holmes McDougall.

Slater, J. (1989) *The Politics of History Teaching: a humanity dehumanised* Special Professorial Lecture. London: Institute of Education, University of London.

Taylor, C. (1989) *Sources of the Self: the making of the modern identity.* Cambridge: Cambridge University Press.

Walsh, W. H. (1951, 3rd expanded ed 1967) *An Introduction to Philosophy of History.* London: Hutchinson.

Weil, S. (1958) 'The Iliad, A Poem of Force', in *Intimations of Christianity among the Ancient Greeks.* Boston: Beacon Press.

Weil, S. (tr.1962) *Selected Essays 1934-1943.* Oxford: Oxford University Press.

White, J. (1982) *The Aims of Education Restated.* London: Routledge and Kegan Paul.

White, J. (1990) *Education and the Good Life: beyond the National Curriculum.* London: Kogan Page in association with the Institute of Education, University of London.

NOTES ON THE AUTHORS

Peter Lee has taught history in comprehensive, secondary modern and direct-grant grammar schools. His research interests are in the philosophy of history and children's understanding of history. He was a Co-Director of the Cambridge History Project from its inception in 1985 and remains a Consultative Director. His books include *History teaching and historical understanding* (1978) and *Learning history* (1984), both with Angela Dickinson. He is currently engaged in research on concepts of history and teaching approaches at Key Stages 2 and 3 of the National Curriculum.

John Slater was HM Staff Inspector for history from 1974 to 1987 and from 1988 to 1990 was a Visiting Professor at the Institute of Education, University of London.

Denis Shemilt is Head of the Department of History at Trinity and All Saints College, Leeds. He was an evaluator and Director of the Schools Council project *History 13-16* was a Co-Director of the Cambridge History Project from its inception in 1985 to 1990 and remains a Consultative Director. His publications include *History 13-16 evaluation study* (1980) and The Devil's locomotive, *History and Theory*, 22 (1983).

Paddy Walsh is a Senior Lecturer in curriculum studies at the Institute of Education, University of London. His special fields are philosophy, curriculum theory and religious education.

John White is Professor of Philosophy at the Institute of Education, University of London. His publications include *Towards a compulsory curriculum*, (1973); *The aims of education restated* (1982); and *Education and the good life: Beyond the National Curriculum* (1990).